Let These Stones Live

Let These Stones Live

A Christian Guide to the Holy Land

James M. Houston

REGENT COLLEGE PUBLISHING
Vancouver, British Columbia

Let These Stones Live
Copyright © 2021 James M. Houston

Regent College Publishing
5800 University Boulevard
Vancouver, BC V6T 2E4 Canada

All rights reserved. No part of this publication may be reproduced, stored in a retrieval system, or transmitted, in any form or by any means, electronic, mechanical, photocopying, recording or otherwise, without the prior written permission of the author, except in the case of brief quotations embodied in critical articles and reviews.

Regent College Publishing is an imprint of the Regent Bookstore (RegentBookstore.com). Views expressed in works published by Regent College Publishing are those of the author and do not necessarily represent the official position of Regent College (Regent-College.edu).

ISBN: 978-1-57383-577-0

Front cover photo: Pontus Wellgraf, courtesy Unsplash.com
Back cover photo of Dr. Houston: Bronwyn Spilsbury, October 2018

Contents

Foreword / vii

Preface / ix

Introduction / 1

1. Topo-history of Old Testament Saints / 7

2. The Birth and Ministry of Jesus / 9

3. The Galilean Ministry of Jesus / 11

4. Paul's Missionary Travel / 21

Conclusion / 25

Foreword

As I read Dr. Houston's words about the tectonic shifts that shaped and formed the biblical coastline, my mind returned to that sunshiny day when we stood at Caesarea Maritima and I asked, "Dr. Houston would you like to share anything here?"

Most pilgrim groups in that location talk about Pontius Pilate, who had a base there, or about Herod the Great, who built the harbour. They might speak of Peter meeting Cornelius there, or of Paul boarding a ship to spread the gospel. But when Dr. Houston opened his mouth, he spoke of shifting tectonic plates, deep undersea movements from which evolved the wonders of biblical history. It was a first!

This is because Dr. Houston's mind encompasses the vast territories not only of geography, whether human or physical, but also history, including pre-human history. Undergirding it all is geology, the foundations of the earth, and he combines it into an expression of God's great love, experienced still today, in real time and place.

Our group, made up mostly of Regent College alumni, smiled to hear his words! This was what we came for: the vast knowledge and yet the intimate spiritual reality that formed our pilgrimage.

The moments were precious and timeless. On a hill overlooking the Sea of Galilee, Dr. Houston reflected on the Psalmist David, whose words shaped the imagination of our Shepherd-Messiah. Jesus also walked those hills and sailed on that Sea. Later, in Jerusalem, we received his reflections on the crucifixion and the garden resurrection. He took us to stories as deep as any tectonic shift—and deeper yet—like the deep magic of Narnia.

It was a journey beyond compare. A geographical-historical-spiritual-intellectual pilgrimage of heart, mind, and strength. Through it, Dr. Houston taught us to know and love the Lord our God more widely and more personally, according to the Great Command. Through it we also came to love our fellow travellers more wholly and fearlessly. Those relationships continue. That is Dr. Houston's way—the pilgrim way.

We were all the better for it, as I know the readers of this book—which covers an even broader scope—will be too.

Let These Stones Live

On our journey Dr. Houston declared, "The threads of my life came together here," as lectures unspoken for fifty years (such as tectonic shifts) blended with the spiritual theology and friendships he has cultivated since. We are all grateful to be woven into his story, and into the tapestry of glory.

May this book be a gift of wisdom such as the magi brought to Bethlehem, in honour of the Lord Jesus, who became the Cornerstone.

Bronwyn Spilsbury
Director/Pastor, Pilgrim Way
www.pilgrimway.ca

Preface

Without the invitation of Bronwyn Spilsbury to join her on a pilgrimage to the Holy Land, this booklet would never have been written. I am indebted also to Regent College Publishing and to our alumni Tze-Hung and Rosemary Perera for the photos.

James M. Houston
March 2021

Introduction

This is a guidebook of the spiritual history of Christianity. It covers such a very small territory, contrasted with the vast continental dimensions of China. Yet it is so dense in its historical significance. While Confucian culture relates all things to a correspondence with "heaven" in all its mysterious magnitude, only a few hundred kilometers contain all the history of the Christian Bible. Contrastive again, while "correspondence with heaven," is vastly abstract, the topographical history of the Bible is intimately specific and personal. Just reading and reflecting on this one paragraph is so difficult to some Asian mindsets and cultures.

That is why we are taking you on a journey through history, for intrinsically, Christianity is enacted within topographical history. In this very small area of the world, the Biblical men and women lived. Even on the very stones Jesus stood, and taught his disciples, we can stand there today! No other religions have such specificity, or such personal encounter with us today.

Religious Life Is a Pilgrimage

The fundamental and all-encompassing theme of the spiritual life is pilgrimage, whether Christian, Buddhist, or Islamic. Its images are of wayfaring, of exile and repatriation, of alienation and reconciliation, and of journeys through the wilderness to gain the promised land.

The Incarnation and the Mystery of the Trinity Are a Pilgrimage

The Bible abounds with these images, from the paradise of Eden in Genesis, to the city of God in the book of Revelation. In the incarnation, Jesus himself embodies this narrative, in his life, death, and resurrection. Profoundly Robert D. Crouse states,

> Pilgrimage is the very life of God himself. The holy Trinity. The out-going of God the Father in his own self-knowing, which is the eternal begetting of his Word; and the eternal procession of God the Holy Spirit, whereby the knower and the known are bound in mutual love. Thus, the very name of God, as love, bespeaks the timeless pilgrimage of God. What, then, is man's imaging of God, but a timely

limitation of that eternal pilgrimage? What is man's vocation, but the call to take the pilgrim's way, to be caught up in the drawing of that supernal triune love which (as Dante puts it) "moves the sun and the other stars."[1]

No wonder, pilgrimage to Jerusalem has shaped the history of the church. "For they that say such things seek a country" (Heb. 11:14).

Inspiring Pilgrims

During the reign of Constantine, his Christian mother, Helena, traveled to Palestine to restore the Christian sites that we can visit today. Helena authorized a remarkable reconstruction of the holy places with the power of Caesar. Previously Caesar had crucified our Lord—an ironic turn of history!

Another remarkable woman, Princess Birgitta (1303–1373), was the sister of the Swedish monarch in the fourteenth century. A visit to her palace, which she converted into a convent, much inspired me years ago. Alone, she left the palace to spend many years traveling by sea and land, first to Rome, and then to Jerusalem. She returned to reform the faith of her country.

But we corrupt all good things, even pilgrimage, as Chaucer's *Canterbury Tales* poignantly exposes. For medieval pilgrimage became a tax dodge for those in debt. A pilgrim would have all his or her debts removed by becoming a pilgrim. Earlier, the crusades had been another mixed motive for conquering and restoring the holy sites. The Knights Templar even introduced Sufi mysticism into Italian Catholic life!

Crossroads of the Ancient World

God our Creator had a divine purpose in choosing a particular place and time where and when God differentiated man from the animals, to bear the *imago dei*. *Homo sapiens* migrating from the Rift Valley of West Africa, encountered *Neanderthal* man who evolved from Europe across the edge of the Continental ice, as far as

---

1. Robert D. Crouse, *Images of Pilgrimage: Paradise and Wilderness in Christian Spirituality* (St. Peter Publications, 1986).

Siberia. The details I describe in an as-yet unfinished book. *Homo sapiens* was more conflictual, learning to speak, whereas Neanderthal was more communal, learning to communicate with music. The latter began as evidenced by cave drawings to have a sense of transcendence, which was heightened in the Near East, profoundly so in Egypt.

Much later, Palestine became the crossroads of trading routes: *Via Maris*, or "the Way of the Sea," dating from the early Bronze Age, linking Egypt with the northern empires of Syria, Anatolia, and Mesopotamia. The name is from the Vulgate of Matthew 4:15 and Isaiah 9:1.

The King's Highway began in Egypt and stretched across the Sinai Peninsula to Aqaba. This was the route on which Joseph was sold to the Midianite traders into Egypt. Traversing the Jordan River, it leads to Damascus and the Euphrates River.

"The Way of the Patriarchs" is a ridge road that crosses the Valley of Jezreel. To the west is the northern tip of the Plain of Sharon, near Caesarea Maritima, and the route extends to the north of the Sea of Galilee with Megiddo right in the middle, controlling the connection between the two main ancient routes.

Geology and Tectonics

Tectonics have shaped the coastline of Palestine, as well as the dramatic trough of the Dead Sea. Abram had a warning from God to flee with his nephew Lot from Sodom and Gomorrah, as these cities perished in an earthquake. Recently, it was discovered that in Jurassic times, a meteor slammed into the Dead Sea area to create this deep trough, 1000 meters below sea level. Mount Carmel, too, is a tectonic block, rising dramatically above the coast.

Was the exodus coincidental with a great earthquake that temporarily blocked the Red Sea itself, so that the Israelites "crossed on dry land"? Perhaps. Much earlier, was Noah's flood caused by tectonic blockage of the Black Sea, only to be opened subsequently in the narrow strait of the Dardanelles, to create the flooding of the Black Sea basin, from the waters pouring in from the Mediterranean? Was it then on Turkish forested slopes that

Noah built his ark?

It is also significant that probably the origin of domesticated grapes occurred in the mountains of Georgia, on whose coast Noah may have disembarked . . . and got drunk! Much later, there is evidence of an early wine trade from Georgia to Greece, which may explain the voyage of Ulysses. All intriguing questions! Doubtless, too, thermal springs of water on the northeast side of the Sea of Galilee, feeding nutrients and warm water, may explain "the right place" where Jesus ordered the disciples to haul up the huge catch of fish.

Limestone, the Alter Ego of the Palestinian Landscapes

Cretaceous and Jurassic limestones are the alter ego of the Palestinian landscapes, so contrasted to the ancient geological rocks of the peninsula of Mount Sinai. They also form much of the steep mountains of China. These limestones, with rich aquifers, explain the numerous wells fed by springs described in the Bible. Cisterns provided stored water within the walled towns against prolonged sieges, notably Jerusalem, but also for chariot fortress towns like Megiddo. The cistern was a pear-shaped reservoir, lined with clay that was in use after the thirteenth century BC. Many are still in use! But an earthquake could crack and destroy the capacity for water storage of a cistern; hence Jeremiah's imagery of an apostate people, being like a useless, fissured cistern "that can hold no water!" (Jer. 2:13).

The domestication of the horse, harnessed to a light chariot for a warrior, was like the "atom bomb" of the ancient world. This new weaponry enabled vast territories to be captured swiftly and for new empires to be created. This occurred at the end of the Bronze Age, when the melting of iron and copper and tin produced a harder yet lighter metal for weaponry.

The rivers of the Near East—the Nile, Euphrates, and Tigris—explain the hydraulic civilizations that became great empires surrounding and threatening the tiny community of Israelites, as Christians still feel threatened today. The Indus hydraulic civilization, arising in the delta of the Indus around 28,000 BC, was the first. Then followed the hydraulic civilizations of the Hwang Ho and Yangtze in China. These became interconnected by Chinese trade across the Indian Ocean to trade with Egypt.

Massive organization of labor to build dams and irrigation was necessary to water the first grain crops of the Neolithic Revolution. In turn, these food crops stabilized households and family life, the source of further human inventiveness, with the use of fire at the family hearth. Our household churches today provide the ongoing resilience of Christian faith that empires cannot destroy. They did not destroy the faith of Abraham, though even he did compromise on one occasion when he pretended his wife was his sister before the preying eyes of the pharaoh of his time. The Israelites later also languished in Egypt, but as Daniel knew in the lion's den, "our God is able to deliver us!"

Our party witnessed in the soft Cretaceous limestone the hollow site where the boy David faced the giant Goliath (1 Sam. 17:1–11) in the Valley of Elah. He ran down from the ridge of Jurassic limestone, with its scattering of small rocks and stones, and picking up five for his sling shot, killed Goliath. Even as we stood there, Israelite aircraft roared overhead as a Hamas missile, hurtling over our heads, struck a nearby hamlet. On the Jurassic ridge, from which David ran to meet Goliath, is now a missile site, demonstrating the story of David and Goliath is still being played out!

Instead of following the geographical places in sequence, we shall follow the historical events with landscape views to help us.

Where Abraham Lived

The flocks and wells where Abraham fed his flocks were in what is now southern

Palestine. The limited rainfall of Beersheba made ownership of the wells of water a critical factor of wealth. At Beersheba, Abraham made a treaty with Abimelech (Gen. 21:17). Some 40 kilometers away, or "two days' journey," is Mount Moriah, where Abraham was willing to sacrifice his son in being tested by God (Gen. 22:1–19). From there, Abraham returned to Beersheba. Later, we find Abraham fleeing with Lot from Sodom and Gomorrah to the headstreams of the Jordan. His travels indicate he was mapping out the location of the Holy Land for the rest of Old Testament history.

Moses' territory reflects displacement and emancipation, rather than possession, in contrast to that of Abraham. He exemplifies the identification of the Israelites as a "redeemed people" being prepared spiritually to occupy the Land of Promise. His critical event is at Mount Sinai. There he was equipped by God to lead in the redemption of God's people.

David's citadel of Mount Zion later reflects a permanent temple of worship, no longer the wandering tabernacle. All is now focused on the temple he built at Jerusalem. That centralization of worship continued until the destruction of the temple in AD 70, after the death and resurrection of Christ. Then the worship of God no longer has a geographical locale, for now it is in the hearts of Christians throughout the whole world. The embodiment of faith has forever replaced the holy places of previous history. Christ now dwells in our hearts by faith! Nevertheless, Christian truth is, as we shall see, contained in topographical history.

1

Topo-History of Old Testament Saints

The Call of Abraham

We enter into biblical history with the call of Abraham to leave his household gods, "to serve the living and true God." He and his family and flocks of sheep traveled widely, from Ur, on the lower Euphrates river, to Harran, beyond the upper Euphrates (Gen. 12:1), in what is now Syria. Then he moved from Aleppo, via Ebla and Damascus, to the coastal road into Egypt (Gen. 12:10–20). Then he was tested to offer his son Isaac as a sacrifice on Mount Moriah (Gen. 22). This site is a volcanic plug rimmed by a Jurassic ridge. It features rough thickets suitable as firewood for burning on the sacrificial altar. The lamb then for the sacrifice has to be carried from a distance, hence Isaac's perplexity in asking his father, "The fire and the wood are here . . . but where is the lamb for the burnt offering?" (Gen. 22: 5). How agonizing that question was—it would have haunted a beloved father for the rest of his life! The lamb was heard bleating, caught in the thickets of the Jurassic ridge.

Yet even the faith of the father of the faithful sometimes faltered. The beauty of his wife Sarah was a danger over which Abraham's faith in God was twice tested: with Abimilech, king of Gerar, then with the pharaoh of Egypt (Gen. 20:1–18).

The Call of Moses

We may sometimes question why God has chosen us to be his people when we are so inadequate. Then we read about Moses who felt just as we do: wholly inadequate! In ethnicity, he was mixed: born an Israelite, reared as an Egyptian. He was compassionate about the slavery of his kinsmen, the Israelites, but what could a single youth do against the power of almighty Egypt? No wonder he protested against God's command at the burning bush, feeling just as fragile and combustible as that bush on Mount Sinai! He tries every excuse to avoid the call, to lead the people of Israel out of Egypt. Meanwhile, God had used an unusual high flood of the Nile, to bring an unusual sequence of nine plagues to the lower Nile valley (Exod. 7:14–10:29). Whether it was a burning bush for Moses, or a phenomenal sequence of the flooding of the Nile causing erosion of the soil to make the water "blood colored" or full of frogs and other pestilence, everything was being synchronized by God to deliver his people.

What then, about the crossing of the Red Sea? Tectonics shape the shoreline of the Red Sea. Was there an undersea upheaval of a tectonic block that created a bridge of dry land for the Israelites to escape into the Negev? Was it followed by a tidal wave that swept the Egyptian army into the Red Sea? We do not know. But throughout the history of God's people, there has been the constant awareness of what Daniel the prophet affirmed: "Our God is able to deliver us, but if not, we shall not bow down."

The Pivotal Focus of Mount Zion

In 2 Chronicles 3:1, we read that Solomon began to build the house of the Lord "in Jerusalem, on Mount Moriah." This mountain is only mentioned one other time in the Bible concerning Abraham's willingness to sacrifice Isaac (Gen. 22:2). The city's foundations are soft Cretaceous chalk, with aquifers for stored water, such as built by David and Solomon, with the great slabs of stone for the foundation of the temple quarried on the spot. The walls of Jerusalem have been rebuilt more than once of hard Jurassic limestone. Jerusalem has endured over twenty military sieges—not exactly the city of peace the Israelites have prayed it would be. Its valleys and hills have thus been carved out of the soft Cretaceous and hard Jurassic limestones so characteristic of all the landscapes of Palestine.

At an elevation of 750 meters, its climate is moderate, with an average rainfall of 63 centimeters. This is divided into three seasons: "the early rain" (Deut. 11:14; Jer. 5:25), about the middle of October; "the rain in its season" (Exod. 9:33; 1 Kings 8:33); and "the latter rain" (Hos. 6:3; Jer. 5:24), in January–March. The oscillation of the rain seasons affected the prayer life of the Jews, with intensifying national prayer as the drought worsened!

2

The Birth and Ministry of Jesus

Arriving by air at Tel-Aviv airport, you will find that just to the south is the ancient sea-port of Joppa or Jaffa. The fortress-port already existed in 1435 BC when it was captured by Pharaoh Thutmose III (1490–1435). It remained a key port for many succeeding invasions. After the experience of Pentecost, it was here that Peter had the vision of a net let down from heaven, containing a great variety of fish. His spiritual horizon had to be enlarged, as all Christians still need reminding, to account for the fact that God's dealings with human beings are much vaster than our narrow, tunnel vision.

To the north, on the Via Maritima, is Megiddo. It was strategically situated on a hill overlooking the outlet of a mountain pass connecting the plain of Esdraelon to the coastal plain. Twenty strata of excavations have been made, reaching back to the Middle Bronze Age. The period of the Patriarchs is covered by levels XV to X. Its famous water system has a vertical shaft through the ruins to the bedrock and a deep spring. A large Canaanite temple is below level VI. Megiddo, capital of the province of Megiddo, was a royal chariot city, with vast horse stables, probably established by the Assyrians. It was destroyed by Pharaoh Necho in 609 BC.

Bethlehem

Bethlehem is an ancient site first mentioned in the Amarna Letters (1360–1332 BC). It is the Ephrath of

Genesis 35:19, visited by Jacob and where Rachel died (Gen. 35:16). Justin Martyr mentions the cave where Jesus was thought to be born (cf. Matt. 2:1–16). In the fourth century, Constantine constructed a basilica over a group of caves. Justinian reconstructed and extended Constantine's shrine, with further medieval reconstructions, as acts of piety.

Shepherds' Field

Although not verified, the Shepherd's Field was thought to be where the Hebrew matriarchs Ruth and Naomi gleaned in the fields behind the harvesters on their way to Bethlehem. Ruth married Boaz, and they became ancestors of King David, who was born in Bethlehem. All this is fraught with symbolism, as Ruth became the archetype of Mary, the mother of Jesus. "But thou Bethlehem Ephratah, though thou be little among the thousands of Judah, yet out of thee shall he come forth unto me that is to be ruler in Israel: whose goings forth have been from of old, from everlasting" (Micah 5:2).

3

The Galilean Ministry of Jesus

Known also as the Sea of Gennesaret, of Chinnereth, and of Tiberias, it is c. 33 miles in circumference, 13 miles long and 8.1 miles wide. Its maximum depth is 141 feet. Relatively shallow, its peaceful calm can quickly be transformed by violent storms, as winds funnel through the east-west Galilean hill country, or more violent yet, from the Golan Heights to the east. Jesus once faced such a violent storm with his disciples, a symbol of how he is always with his disciples in their deep troubles!

In a grotto, at the source of the Jordan River, two religious systems were later blended: Pan or Baal was worshiped in the grotto, and Caesar was worshiped on the hill above it. In Roman times, rich confusion between religion and politics prevailed, as numerous Roman coins have been found in the grotto, several depicting the playing of Pan's flute. Could this be where Neanderthal man, who invented the flute much earlier, also worshiped as well? Herod, too, built a temple here. It was on a journey to Caesarea Philippi that Jesus challenged the disciples dramatically: "Who do people say that I am? What about you?" (Mark 8:27, 29).

Golan Heights

Ancient Chalcolithic pastoral settlements have been excavated reaching back to the time of Abraham, but these were intermittent because of numerous invasions.

Saint Peter in Galliacantu

The essay by Marcus Bockmuehl, "Simon Peter: The Transformation of the Apostle," is invaluable.[2] It concludes that probably Peter never was martyred in Rome or buried there, but possibly ended his life where he

---

2. Marcus Bockmuehl, "Simon Peter: The Transformation of the Apostle," in *Sources of Christian Identity*, ed. James M. Houston and Jens Zimmerman (Grand Rapids: Eerdmans, 2018), 69–83.

began a humble fisherman at Bethsaida, a peasant fishing hovel called el-Araj! Prior to Peter's day, Bethsaida had been a Roman fortress, el-Tell, but it lay in ruins in Peter's time. It was the original home of Phillip, Andrew, and his brother Peter. In its environs Jesus fed the five thousand.

Nazareth

"Can any good come out of Nazareth?" It was an ancient village, whose excavations reveal Bronze and Iron Age settlement. The most authentic Christian site is a spring on the north side of the present city, known from the twelfth century as Mary's Well. There are remains of an early church from before the age of Constantine. But the site of the synagogue where Jesus (Luke 4:16–29) preached is in doubt. The reconstruction of a village similar to the time of Jesus has been built, a replica of which is also in the new Bible Museum in Washington, DC.

My favorite meditation is to envisage Jesus learning as a boy the craft of his father, Joseph, as a carpenter. He learned to make good yokes for the animals, ploughing the land. So Jesus claims, "Take my yoke upon you, for my yoke is easy, my burden is light" (Matt. 11:29–30). It was contrastive with "the yoke of oppression" frequently described by the prophets. Could the good craftsmanship Jesus showed, key to the whole rural economy, have been so reliable that it would have been easy to trust his mysterious invitation to "take my yoke upon you"?

The wedding feast at Cana is where Jesus performed his first miracle (John 2:1–11). In the National Art Museum in Paris, there is a spectacular seventeenth-century painting of this miracle that the crowds never see, because it backs the rather ugly painting of the Mona Lisa, which the world wants to see! But the eager eyes of joy and celebration are wonderfully depicted.

Beit She'an

To-day, in the national park of Beit She'an visitors can view this Roman city built for retired Roman troops, similar to Milan, another city for veteran troops. Fifteen different levels of civilization were built over each other across the centuries. Renamed Scythopolis in 63 BC, "city of the Scythians," it became the capital of the Decapolis, the only one on the west bank of the Jordan. It was destroyed by an earthquake in AD 749.

Jericho

One of the oldest cities of the Near East (over nine thousand years old), it originated in a fort in the Bronze Age. Why is this story so particularized in the book of Joshua, when small skirmishes were frequently taking place? Biblically, it is because it is the site of the first victory of a new leader, Joshua, as the successor to Moses. That his small army was to march around the city walls seven times was symbolic of other ceremonial processes, all expressive of obedience to God. Morally, we find it abhorrent at the apparent thousands of enemies always being killed at God's command. But the Israelites had to learn that their coming Messiah loves righteousness and hates iniquity. There can be no assimilation with the enemies of God. The sin of Achan, in hiding his booty taken from the enemy, was that of compromise, punishable by God (Josh. 7:1–26).

Symbolically, the modern Israelites built their first settlement beyond the Zionist border, at Ariel, just below Mount Ebal, near where Joshua's tomb is located. It is a modern statement that Joshua is the iconic leader of modern politics in Israel. Outside Ariel, friends of mine, Mr. and Mrs. Johnson, have constructed a Christian youth camp for training Israel's youth in cooperative physical skills. Secular Israel accepts it as their official youth training camp.

Qumran

There is too much to say on this complex topic, and so I would suggest reading or taking courses from scholars at Trinity Western University, British Columbia, who have specialized on the Qumran Scrolls. The Israel Museum in Jerusalem has a magnificent pavilion, "The Shrine of the Book," where the Dead Sea Scrolls from Qumran are on permanent exhibit.

Masada

It is well worth the climb to this fortress town, where the Jews defied Roman troops after the fall of Jerusalem in AD 70. Herod the Great had built it in AD 31–37. Recent excavations have uncovered a synagogue and the well-preserved mosaic floors of Herod's fortress palace.

On the way to Jerusalem, up the steep road climbing up from the Dead Sea, modern pilgrims are on the road where the Good Samaritan attended the robbed and wounded pilgrim.

Mount of Beatitudes

The sermon that Jesus preached here is recorded in Matthew 5–7 and Luke 6. The apparent discrepancy between Matthew's account as on "a hill," and Luke's narrative as being "a plain," is easily reconciled, as it is a topography of rolling hills of Pliocene limestone and Cretaceous level lands of Miocene limestone. At the intersection of the two is where Jesus stood to preach. The site is commemorated by the Franciscan Monastery, since St. Francis later sought to follow the beatific life.

Meditation on the Beatitudes

As a young man, Jesus summarizes here his own reflections on the Old Testament Scriptures that guided his own Messianic consciousness. He is anticipating a new Israel in a new covenant. It expresses *germinal precis*, the coming of the kingdom of God that the apostles later preached. It concludes the Old Testament of Judaism with a new covenant, expressing the constant admonition of the Old Testament: "Obey, then you will live" (Latin *obaudire*, meaning "listen!"). It includes "The Golden Rule" of the Old Testament, the heart of the Torah, quoted in Matthew 7:12: "So whatever you wish that men should do unto you, do so to them: for this is the law and the prophets." But Jesus uses it differently from the negative usage of the Hillel—"You shall not do harm to your neighbor." Positively, Jesus says: "The love which you yourself would experience, you should show to your neighbor." In the statements of the Sermon on the Mount, there are no parallels in the Talmud, for they are decisive sayings, said with authority.

A Jewish stranger hearing Jesus speak could only respond that this is the antithesis of all Jewish teaching—blasphemy! Reporting this to the temple officials was the beginning of the cry, "Crucify Him!" Meditate on this, that with the Sermon on the Mount, Jesus is already embracing the cross. But as Christians, we too react, "This is an impossible ideal!" It is a perfectionism we cannot live! Only much later could the four evangelists, meditating over their own life experience of being constantly with Jesus, come to understand the Sermon on the Mount. As Henry Scougal was to write centuries later, it is having "the life of Jesus in the soul of man." They are isolated sayings that Jesus made into a garment of holiness. They became mission statements for the disciples and ourselves to preach and live by. This is the way of life, of being a disciple of Christ.

But the consequences of expressing such divine love did, does, and always will generate hate and persecution. Yet this gospel is not law. Rather they delineate the depth, length, and breadth of the Christian Gospel and of the love of God. Can we ever fully understand and live the Sermon on the Mount? Never! Are we, as tourists, just visiting the Mount of the Beatitudes? Or do we dwell frequently in a Franciscan church, like the one built in 1939, on the Mount of the Beatitudes, in unceasing worship?

Jerusalem

The Garden of Gethsemane (meaning "oil vat" in Aramaic) was a garden of olives. Within it is the traditional "rock of the agony," first identified by the pilgrim Arcuif. The olive trees may well have had their origins at least by the seventh century BC. Again, this is not a tourist site, but a place of holy meditation: "My Father, if it is not possible for this cup to be taken away unless I drink it, may your will be done" (Matt. 26:36–56; Mark 14:32–50; Luke 22:39–53; John 18:1–14).

The Upper Room

It is on a site considered to have been where many other events are recorded in the Gospels: the washing of the disciples' feet (John 13); post-resurrection appearances (John 20); the gathering of the disciples after the ascension (Acts 1:13); the election of Matthias as apostle (Acts 1:26); and the descent of the Holy Spirit at Pentecost (Acts 2:1).

The Trial, Death, and Resurrection of Jesus

We tend to see the scourged and bleeding Jesus as a victim, instead of being in fact in charge of his own rejection. For as the Savior of the world he was in charge, not his enemies. Then, when on the cross he said, "It is finished," more was done than our salvation. The creator's intent that humans should bear the *imago dei* was completed. Our pious compassion for Jesus is not big enough to see the whole of God's purpose in the incarnation. This makes our visit to the various temples and churches rather irksome: to see how diverse church traditions have narrowed our meditations on the trial and death of Jesus to ecclesial politics!

Just as there are differing systems of law today, such as Chinese or Western systems, so it was in the conquered land of ancient Palestine. Crimes had to be counterbalanced by punishments, and the death sentence was carried out in autumn and winter, the seasons of decay and death in nature. The Sanhedrin, which served as the Jewish legal court, was established in 191 BC. It had a president, vice president, and sixty-nine members settling matters of religious law by a majority vote. But around AD 28 the Sanhedrin was stripped of its right to try capital offenses. The arrest of Jesus now required six different trials—three with the Jewish courts and three with the Roman authorities, in order to convict and sentence him to death.[3]

The Garden of the Resurrection

A guide will explain why this site we visited may be the site where the risen Lord revealed himself; my brief comment is about how hard it was for them to believe. Belief and conception are twins. If you do not conceive something is possible, you will never look to see where and how it may happen. It was so with the disciples. John is the beloved disciple who believed all things were possible with his beloved Lord. He narrates how he himself saw the evidence in the tomb. "He saw and believed" (John 20:8). Peter and the other disciples did not! Mark's Gospel, linked with the narrative of Peter, sees an angel in the empty tomb, but he does not see the evidence like John; his narrative is more external, not from the heart like John's is. Reflect where you are as a Christian—more empirical and practical, or more contemplative, like the women around Jesus, who just adored their Lord?

Mount Zion

The Domitian Abbey, built to house the monks protecting the Upper Room and the Tomb of David, is named from the Latin word *domitio*, or "falling asleep." It commemorates the Roman Catholic belief that Mary the mother of Jesus did not die but fell asleep and was carried up into heaven. The book of Samuel records that Mount Zion, called the stronghold of Zion, was the Jebusite fortress, mentioned in Isaiah 60:14 and frequently in the Psalms.

David's Tomb

David was buried c. 1000 BC, south of the present walled city, as narrated by 1 Kings 2:10 and Nehemiah 3:16. Traditionally, it is near the site of the Byzantine church, Hagia Zion.

---

3. Seth Pollinger, *The World Jesus Knew* (Museum of the Bible, 2017), 108–21, gives a vivid amplification of the trial narratives of the Gospels.

Destruction of the Temple, Devastation of the Palestinan Economy

Pilgrims visiting Jerusalem will be conducted underground to the corner-stone of the temple mount. Comparable to the huge block in the port of Capernaum, its Roman technology is amazing. The prophetic utterance that no one stone will remain upon another was true of the building, but not its foundation.

Famines have been a frequent event in the Near East. It occurred in the time of Jacob, and it was always due to the failure of either the autumnal or the early rains. But there is no evidence of climate change in biblical times, as I wrote an essay to the Victoria Institute in 1947, checking that all the fruits mentioned at different places in the biblical texts are still where they were grown. The last famine we know of occurred in the reign of Claudius, or again in the reign of Nero. Queen Helena of Adiabene on a pilgrimage to Jerusalem found the city in famine. She had grain and figs imported from Alexandria through Caesarea around 45 BC.

Famine brings wealth to some and poverty to the masses. Joseph of Arimathea may have been one of those wealthy families who provided the family vault for Jesus' body. Nicodemus came from another wealthy family. The Great Revolt in AD 70 was probably more about money than political freedom!

With the destruction of the Temple, the whole Palestinian economy collapsed. It put into unemployment around 18,000 workers building the Temple and its roads of access. Far more serious, the whole regional economy was profoundly affected, with no market for all the sheep, bullocks, and doves. All the sheep country covering Israel was affected. The Great Revolt led to the Roman confiscation of large tracts of land in Judea belonging to the rebels. The whole Jewish society was destabilized. No wonder the apostle Paul was aroused to raise funds from the churches of his ministry in Asia Minor, to bring in funds to relieve the distress of their fellow Christians in Israel!

But there was also a great religious revolution that is vividly described by the great preacher of the epistle to the Hebrews: now there is no more need for the sacrifice of animals. The Temple worship is abolished, and a new worship has begun with the final sacrifice for sin, Christ our Lord. So radical was this moral revolution that even the pagan Roman philosophers, the Stoics, now advocated that pagan animal sacrifice was no longer to be practiced. Moral accountability is to be faced directly, as man for man. This is now the new context of the preacher/teacher: uniting the epistle to the Hebrews with the destruction of the Temple!

Peter's New Ministry

"Lord, what about him?" (John 21:21). Little did Peter realize, when he was forgiven by the Lord for His denial, how contrasted would be his role from that of Saul of Tarsus or his fellow apostle John. "The kind of death he should die" would be that of becoming hidden in his birthplace, carrying on as a fisherman while John would travel to Asia Minor, prominent in the growing churches there. Peter was first shown whole new potentials in his dream at Jaffa/Caesarea Philippi, only then to be reduced to a minimum of visibility in a hidden life in Bethsaida, where he had grown up!

The Port of Caesarea

This is one of the worst places to build a Palestinian port, as the tidal drift and strong sea winds and currents have littered it with port ruins as far back as the Minoan/Phoenician invaders from Crete in the time of Samson in the book of Judges. But Roman technology had advanced by the time of Herod the Great. Caesarea now gave the Romans an entry and a base to conquer Palestine. Herod spent twelve years (25–13 BC) building the great port. How blocks of Miocene limestone 50 x 10 x 9 feet were ever assembled to build the mole, standing in 180 feet of water, is unknown. All we know is that the Miocene limestone is soft when cut. The sea wall was curved around to form a haven. Then around the foreshore a wall protected the town, its houses, racecourse, amphitheater, and temples.

As a cynical politician, Herod was restoring the temple in Jerusalem for the Jews while building a temple to the worship of Caesar at Caesarea. No wonder the Jews sneered at Pilate at the trial of Jesus, "If you let this man (Jesus) go free you are no friend of Caesar!" (John 19:12). Not even to the monumental cities Herod himself had built would he escape if the trial of Jesus was not "staged" to please Caesar! Yet today, nothing is now left of the Roman town, except the ruins of the aqueduct bringing water from the north.

4

Paul's Missionary Travels

The Apostle Paul's New Mandate

We cannot trace the apostle's sea journeys as we have traced the patriarchs' journeys by land. But we know the dates. His first sea voyage was from Antioch in Syria in AD 46–48 AD, sailing first to Salamis in northeast Crete, overland to the port of Paphos in southwest Crete, to Perga, then overland on Roman roads to Derbe, then to Iconium, back northwestward to Pisidian Antioch, to the south coast of Asia Minor, then by ship from Attalia, and on to Pieria in northern Syria.

Indomitably, Paul then set sail on his second journey. He took Barnabas as a short time companion from Antioch to Crete, then went on alone overland through Cilicia in southwest Asia Minor, via Derbe, Lystra, Pisidian Antioch, north to Nicaea, Troas, across by a short sea voyage to Neapolis, through Macedonia, to visit Thessalonica and Berea, then by sea again, south along the coast of Greece, and to Corinth, the great seaport city.

The impression we might have is that Paul was simply busy traveling and preaching as a young missionary. But Origen, the great biblical scholar of the second century, sees otherwise. Paul was maturing in his own faith, and as he grew, so did his teaching mature and even ripen deeply in his old age. Like "children in the faith," Paul had to deal with being a scandal to the pagans in that Corinthian Christian sisters began to wear no veil over their heads, seemingly acting like prostitutes; or that meat sold that had been offered to the idols was offensive to the young Christian community. The Corinthian Christians were behaving like teenagers in the faith!

In Paul's third missionary journey, he traveled overland in AD 53–57, visiting Lystra, Derbe, Pisidian Antioch, Laodicea, and Ephesus, across the Dardanelles from Troas, to Philippi, then down the Greek coast by land to Athens and Corinth. His speech on Mars Hill demonstrates how sophisticated he had become in Greek culture, amazing even their philosophers by quoting an obscure Greek poet. Likewise, his deepening awareness of the mystery of the Triune God is expressed in his epistles to the Colossians and Ephesians. The apostle is now a truly a mature Christian addressing mature converts in the faith.

Back in Palestine, Paul was now brought to trial in the colosseum of Caesarea Philippi, the place where earlier on, Peter's eyes had been opened to see Christianity as a global faith. Now Paul had demonstrated it was indeed a gospel for all the world. Appealing to Caesar, Paul is now sent as a "prisoner of the Lord"—not of Caesar's—by a grain ship, following the winds and tidal currents northward to Antioch, then calling briefly at Myra on the south coast of Asia Minor, to Malta, where the ship is shipwrecked in a storm, eventually sailing through the Messina Straits to Puteoli, the seaport of Rome. Here Paul met more ethnically sophisticated Christians and wrote a mature missionary epistle about a global gospel, the epistle to the Romans, for both Jews and Gentiles.

It was Paul's dream to go the limits of the Mediterranean Sea: Spain. Did he ever reach there? We also know that a very large number of the population bear Jewish names, traceable to the ancient copper mines in Rio Tinto. We do not know. But we know his dream was passed to later Jewish Christians, who populated Southern Spain in the Visigothic period. This Jewish influence is traceable right up to the sixteenth century when great Christian saints like Teresa of Avila and scholars like Luis de Leon were to generate a Christian Reformation movement in Spain and Italy quite independent of the Reformation of Luther and Calvin.

Mount Carmel and the Carmelite Order

Paul's desire to visit Spain was reversed in the first Crusade of Western Christians desiring to return to Israel. Accompanying them were women, acting as nurses, for the soldiers wounded in battle. After the withdrawal of the crusaders back to Europe, some women stayed on, establishing a small convent on Mount Carmel. It overlooks the seacoast from which Paul sailed on his missionary journeys.

Elevated as a tectonic block, Mount Carmel

rises steeply to some 1500 ft. Its association with thunderstorms is the origin of the Canaanite worship of Baal, the storm god. It explains why in years of drought the Israelites were constantly tempted to worship Baal. At Mt. Carmel, Elijah challenged Baal worship (2 Kings 1:9). Ha-Carmel, meaning "the garden-land," is celebrated as the symbol of beauty in the Song of Songs 7:5 and of fertility in Isaiah 35:2 and Micah 7:14. For the fruits of Carmel "to wither" is the sign of great judgment and catastrophe (Isa. 33:9; Jer. 4:26; Amos 1:2; Nahum 1:4).

In the foothills of Mt. Carmel, a Swedish monastery echoes the pilgrimage of their Princess Birgitta. Both ladies, Birgitta and Teresa, generated profound reformations in their countries of Sweden and Spain. Such is what God does, not by human power but by his Spirit.

Conclusion

In summary, this book is a unique attempt to integrate not just the topography of the Holy Land with its archaeological sites and ancient route ways but also its geology. For it is its tectonics that shape its topographical landscapes, and it is the interface of its Miocene and Pliocene limestones that locate with precision where actual events took place. Now we can envisage where the lamb was caught in the Pliocene thickets, ready for Abraham to offer as a burnt sacrifice, in lieu of Isaac, or where David stood on Mount Elah, to slay Goliath.

Off the coast of the northeast Sea of Galilee, we can locate the exact hot spring that still nurtures a multitude of large fish, such as Jesus directed his disciples to catch. In a crowd of pilgrims today, some can stand on the Miocene lowland where Jesus stood to preach "The Sermon on the Plain", and others nearby are standing on the rocky Pliocene, to hear the same sermon, as "The Sermon on the Mount."

The other new contribution is to link biblical events with the study of numismatics (history of coins) and the science of astronomical events. These include "the sign of Jonah," the star of Events, followed by the Magi to visit the birth of Jesus at Bethlehem, and the sun's eclipse at midday, when Jesus died on the cross. Coins issued by Herod Antipas in A.D. 33 are marked with a darkened sun to depict the eclipse, yet with fleets of light, to depict the flares of the sun's surface waves of hot gases, only visible to the human eye in a solar eclipse.

Such integration of new disciplines to demonstrate the accuracy of the biblical record is a new awareness for Christian pilgrims.

www.ingramcontent.com/pod-product-compliance
Lightning Source LLC
Chambersburg PA
CBHW061403090426
42743CB00003B/129